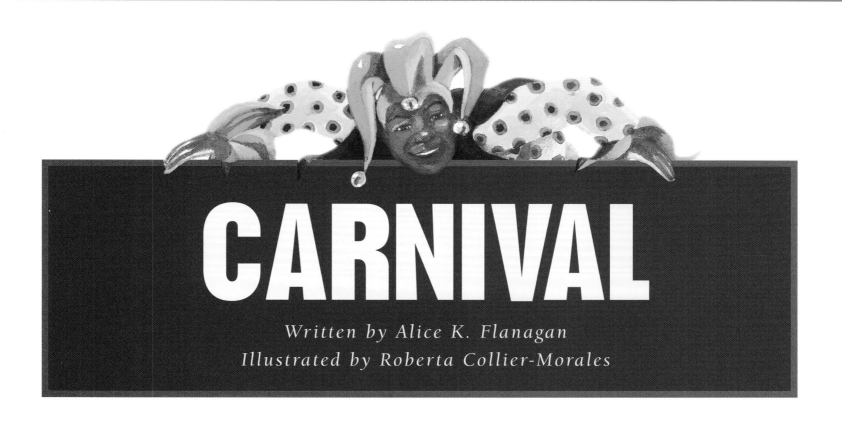

CARNIVAL

Written by Alice K. Flanagan

Illustrated by Roberta Collier-Morales

Content Adviser: Alecia P. Long, Ph.D., Louisiana State Museum, New Orleans, Louisiana

Reading Adviser: Dr. Linda D. Labbo, Department of Reading Education, College of Education, The University of Georgia

COMPASS POINT BOOKS

MINNEAPOLIS, MINNESOTA

Compass Point Books
3109 West 50th Street, #115
Minneapolis, MN 55410

Visit Compass Point Books on the Internet at *www.compasspointbooks.com*
or e-mail your request to *custserv@compasspointbooks.com*

Editors: E. Russell Primm, Emily J. Dolbear, and Patricia Stockland
Designer: The Design Lab

Library of Congress Cataloging-in-Publication Data
Flanagan, Alice K.
  Carnival / written by Alice K. Flanagan ; illustrated by Roberta Collier-Morales ; reading adviser, Linda D. Labbo.
      p. cm. — (Holidays and festivals)
 Includes bibliographical references and index.
  ISBN 0-7565-0478-3 (alk. paper)
  1. Carnival—Juvenile literature. 2. Carnival—United States—Juvenile literature. I. Collier-Morales, Roberta.
II. Labbo, Linda D. III. Title. IV. Series: Holidays and festivals (Compass Point Books)
  GT4180.F53 2004
  394.25—dc21   2002155739

Table of Contents

NOTE: In this book, words that are defined in the glossary are in **bold** *the first time they appear in the text.*

Wear a mask or paint your face. Walk in a parade and dance in the street. It's Carnival time!

People always have fun at Carnival time. They wear costumes and masks and go to parties and parades. The **festival** begins on January 6 and can last four to eight weeks. Carnival is **celebrated** in Europe, the Caribbean islands, and North and South America. The festival has many names. In Italy, it is known as *Carnevale.* It is called *Carnaval* in Mexico. In other countries, it is known as *Carnival.* People in France and the United States call the last day of Carnival *Mardi Gras* (mar-DEE graw). It is known as *Pancake Tuesday* in England. In Germany, it is called *Fastnacht* (Night before the Fast).

How Did
Carnival Begin?

Carnival started hundreds of years ago in Europe. It was a festival to welcome the coming of spring. Farmers prayed that they would have good crops and that their animals would be healthy. Some farmers paraded a fat bull through their villages. Afterward, they held dances and games. Over time, the reason to celebrate the festival changed.

By the ninth century, a new religion had spread throughout Europe. It was called Christianity. Christians believe that Jesus Christ is the Son of God. Many Europeans became Christians. They observed Lent. This was a period of time when they fasted to be like Jesus, who they believed suffered and died for them.

During the fast, they did not eat certain foods such as meat and sweets. In the days before Lent, Christians baked cakes and doughnuts and held parties. They called this time Carnival because this was their last chance to eat what they wanted before Lent. The word "carnival" comes from the Latin words *carne* and *vale,* meaning "goodbye to meat."

What Is Mardi Gras?

The last day of Carnival became special to Christians. The French named it *Mardi Gras,* which means "Fat Tuesday." The day after Mardi Gras is Ash Wednesday. It begins the season of Lent, which lasts for forty weekdays and ends on Easter Sunday.

Easter doesn't always fall on the same date. It can be as early as March 23 or as late as April 25. Because Mardi Gras is always forty-six days before Easter, it can fall on any Tuesday from February 3 to March 9. That's why Carnival, which always begins on January 6 and ends on Mardi Gras, can last anywhere from four to eight weeks, depending on the year. Carnival begins on January 6 to mark the Christian holiday of the Epiphany. Christians believe that three wise men, or possibly three kings, brought gifts to the baby Jesus on January 6, twelve days after he was born.

Mardi Gras in the United States

Carnival and Mardi Gras were not celebrated in the United States until the 1700s. On March 3, 1699, French explorers came to the United States. They sailed down the Mississippi River, stopping at what is now known as Louisiana. Back in France on this same day, people were celebrating Mardi Gras. To remember the festival, the French explorers named the spot where they landed Point du Mardi Gras. Nineteen years later, the city of New Orleans was built nearby. Today, the largest Mardi Gras celebrations in the United States are held in New Orleans.

Modern Mardi Gras celebrations took shape in New Orleans in 1857. That year, six young men formed a Carnival club called Comus. Comus is the name of the Greek god of fun. On the day of the Mardi Gras festivities, the club held a parade. The parade at that time included only two small **floats**. People dressed in costumes and masks and walked behind the floats.

Today, there are many clubs like Comus. They are called **krewes** (crooz). Each krewe holds its own large parade with floats that take a year to build. During the parade, masked people throw plastic beads, plastic cups, and coins to the crowd. These items are called **souvenirs**.

During Carnival, each krewe also holds a large dance called a costume ball. Men and women wear fancy clothes to this festivity. They choose a king and queen to be in charge of all the events.

The Mardi Gras *Courir*

In some parts of Louisiana, people celebrate Mardi Gras much like the poor field workers in France did hundreds of years ago. At that time, winters were hard for people working in the fields. Because they had so little to eat, the workers went from door to door to beg for food from wealthy families. In return for something to eat, they danced, sang songs, and played music.

Today, people relive this custom, which is called the Mardi Gras Courir, or Run. However, they do it for fun. Many put on colorful costumes and ride through the community on horseback. Others travel in wagons and trucks. They stop at farms to ask for gifts of food and money. Many families give chickens, sausage, and rice. In return for the gifts, the riders sing and dance. At the end of the day, they make a stew called gumbo from the food they have collected. Afterward, everyone in the community gathers to eat the food. It is the last feast before Lent begins.

Carnival in Brazil

One of the largest Carnivals in the world takes place in the city of Rio de Janeiro, Brazil. The four-day festival occurs at the end of February or the beginning of March, which is summer in Brazil.

Rio is known for its fancy masked balls and wild street parties. People come from all over the world to hear the brass bands play and to see the parade floats and street performers. There are giant puppets and clowns walking on long poles called **stilts**. The best part of the Rio Carnival is the Samba School parade.

Dancers and musicians train all year to be in the Samba parade. Fourteen schools take part in it. Each Samba School is made up of a group of people from the same neighborhood. They think of a good idea for their floats. Then they make costumes, write songs, and create dances

to go along with that idea. Each Samba School can have six to eight floats in the parade. Sometimes, between three thousand and five thousand people ride on the floats or march alongside them. The best Samba School wins a prize.

Carnival in the Caribbean

French settlers brought Carnival to the Caribbean islands several hundred years ago. At first, only French families on the island celebrated Carnival. Later, African slaves began to celebrate it, too. For them, the festival became a way to forget how hard their lives were. They would dress like their masters and make fun of them. On the islands today, Carnival is still a time for dancing, music, and dressing up.

Celebrations are held on most of the islands at different times. The most famous Carnival celebrations are held in Trinidad and Tobago. People march and dance in the streets to the sounds of steel drums.

Mardi Gras in Canada

Canada is a country north of the United States. It celebrates Carnival during the winter. The most famous Carnival and Mardi Gras is held in Quebec City. It is called *Carnaval de Quebec,* which means "Carnival of Quebec." It lasts for seventeen days and is the third-largest Carnival celebration after those held in Rio de Janeiro and New Orleans.

During Carnaval de Quebec, there are parties, balls, and parades. There are also many winter events that are held outside on the ice and in the snow. The ambassador of the celebration is a snowman called Bonhomme. The city builds an ice palace for him, and he crowns a young woman who is chosen as queen.

Carnaval in Mexico

Mexico is a country south of the United States. It calls its festival Carnaval. During Carnaval, there are parades, fireworks, dancing, and bullfighting. People put on masks and costumes. They dance and join parades. Many dancers dress as cowboys, called *charros*. Others dress

as monkey men (*Maash*). Some dancers become umbrella salesmen (*Paragueros*). They carry huge open umbrellas made of bird feathers.

Mexicans are known for the beautiful masks they carve from wood. Some of the more popular masks resemble the faces of animals such as jaguars, eagles, and coyotes. There are also masks of ancient gods, saints, and Spanish soldiers. Each part of Mexico has its own style of masks.

Things You Might
See During Carnival

Masks

Masks are worn at balls and parades. People wear masks to hide who they are. When they put on a mask, they become someone else. Masks can be scary or silly. Often, it takes many months to make a mask. The people of Mexico carve their masks from wood, but most masks are made of paper, cardboard, cloth, clay, or **papier-mâché.** People decorate them with paint, feathers, shiny stones, glitter, ribbon, and yarn.

Throws or Souvenirs

During parades, some of the people riding on floats throw colorful beads and small toys to the crowd. Many people save these "throws" as souvenirs of the celebration. Float riders have also been known to throw stuffed animals, cards, plastic cups, tokens shaped like early Spanish coins called **doubloons**, and tiny sweet cakes or candy. One of the most popular souvenirs thrown is a decorated coconut.

King Cakes

In New Orleans and Quebec, Canada, "king cakes" are a popular treat during Carnival. King cakes are named for the three kings who visited the baby Jesus in Bethlehem. The cakes are shaped like large doughnuts and are decorated with purple, green, and gold icing. A tiny plastic doll or golden bean is hidden in the cake. It represents the baby Jesus. Whoever gets the piece of cake with the doll or bean in it will have good luck. However, that person must then hold the next party or buy the next king cake.

Gumbo

Gumbo is a meat or seafood stew made with vegetables. It is a popular dish in New Orleans. Okra is the main vegetable in gumbo. Okra comes from West Africa, where it is called *guingombo* (gwin-gum-boh). That is how gumbo got its name. Red peppers are also used in the stew. They give gumbo its hot, spicy flavor. Many people make gumbo with fish. Others use chicken and sausage.

What You Can Do During Carnival

Every year, more cities around the world are joining in the fun of Carnival. They are making this time of year a holiday for everyone. Here are a few things you can do to celebrate Carnival and Mardi Gras.

* Make a silly mask and costume, or paint your face and dress up as a clown. Tell jokes and make people laugh.

* Teach someone to play a game and have fun.

* Do something to entertain others: Play an instrument, do a dance, or sing a song. Get others to sing and dance with you.

* Visit or play with someone who is lonely or sad. Help them forget their troubles.

* Buy or make something that is sweet to eat. Share it with others.

Glossary

celebrated had a party or honored a special event

doubloons old Spanish coins made of gold

fasted went without any food or certain foods, sometimes for religious reasons

festival a holiday or celebration

floats platforms on wheels that carry displays or exhibits in a parade

krewes clubs that organize parades and other festivities to celebrate Mardi Gras and Carnival

Lent the forty weekdays from Ash Wednesday to Easter; a time when Christians fast

papier-mâché paper pulp with glue that makes a light material used for shaping and molding things

souvenirs objects that are kept as reminders of special occasions

stilts long poles with support for the feet partway up so a person can walk high above the ground

Where You Can Learn More about Carnival

At the Library

Hoyt-Goldsmith, Diane, and Lawrence
    Migdale. *Mardi Gras: A Cajun Country
    Celebration*. New York: Holiday House,
    1995.
Keep, Linda Lowery. *Mardi Gras Mix Up*.
    New York: Random House, 1999.
Vidrine, Beverly B., and Patrick Soper.
    A Mardi Gras Dictionary. Gretna, La.:
    Pelican Publications, 1995.

On the Web

Free Kids Crafts
http://freekidscrafts.com/mardi_gras_crafts.htm
For crafts and recipes in celebration of Mardi
Gras, as well as links to other sites

The Holiday Spot
http://theholidayspot.com/mardigras/mask.htm
For directions on how to make your own
Mardi Gras mask

Through the Mail

Louisiana Department of Tourism
P.O. Box 94291
Baton Rouge, LA 70804
225/342-8100
For information about Carnival celebrations

On the Road

Mardi Gras Museum
2309 Ship's Mechanic Row
Galveston, TX 77550
409/765-5930
To see colorful displays, costumes, and exhibits
from Galveston's Carnival celebrations

Mardi Gras World
233 Newton Street
New Orleans, LA 70114
800/362-8213
504/361-7821
To view props, giant figures, and sculptures

Index

About the Author and Illustrator

Alice K. Flanagan writes books for children and teachers. Since she was a young girl, she has enjoyed writing. She has written more than seventy books. Some of her books include biographies of U.S. presidents and their wives, biographies of people working in our neighborhoods, phonics books for beginning readers, and informational books about birds and Native Americans. Alice K. Flanagan lives in Chicago, Illinois.

Roberta Collier-Morales has been a professional illustrator since 1979. She graduated from Colorado State University and received a master's degree from Marywood University in Pennsylvania. She lives in Boulder, Colorado.